The world needs a little more kindness.

Copyright © 2024 Stacy Reubenson and Mira Reubenson

All rights reserved.

No part of this book may be reproduced or transmitted in any form or by any means, electronic or mechanical, including photocopying, recording, or by any information storage and retrieval system, without permission in writing from the copyright owner.

The moral right of the author and illustrator has been asserted.

Copyright © 2024 Stacy Reubenson and Mira Reubenson

ISBN: 978-0-7961-7238-9

First Print: June 2024

Contact: stacyreuby@gmail.com

Author: Stacy Reubenson

Illustrations: Mira Reubenson

Special thanks to:

Rael Reubenson, Jake Reubenson, Diane Goldberg, Lisa Letord, Jo Selbst, Jarred Selbst, Gail Ezekiel

and to our biggest fans
Oli, Jake, Ben & Zevi.

The Kindness Kitty

Stacy & Mira Reubenson

Being kind is something anyone can do,
you can be kind to someone, and they can be kind to you.

You can be kind to someone that you really adore,
and you can be kind to someone you've never met before.

When someone is unkind it's a real pity,
that is when they need...

The Kindness Kitty.

The Kindness Kitty can help people see,
just how easy being kind can be.

There is a little town, not very far away,
the people there are rude and grumpy every single day.

They spend their days whining and groaning,
you would think they are only happy
when they are moaning.

The Kindness Kitty came to this town,
she saw what was going down.

She watched a bit and shed a tear,
"I think they're going to need me here!"

This is Tom, he's a very mean guy,
he likes to make other kids cry.

He teases them, he's nasty and rude,
he puts his teacher in a very bad mood.

Then just like that, straight out of the blue,
a voice said, "Would you like it if someone did that to you?"

"Who is that?" Tom screamed as loud as he could,
"I am the Kindness Kitty" she said, and there she stood.

"I want to show you that you can be kind,
you just need to change your state of mind."

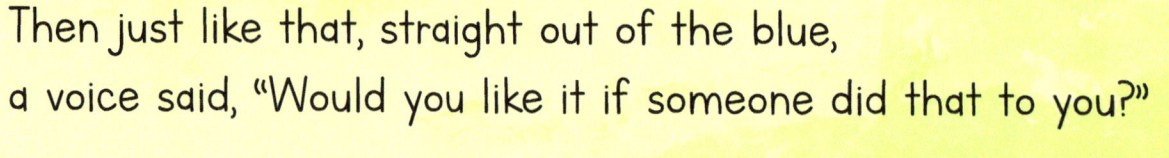

"If you treat people well it will make their day,
you don't even need to go out of your way."

Just as Tom turned his back,
a little girl fell and dropped her snack.

"I don't like to be kind!" Tom cried,
but the Kindness Kitty was cute, so he just tried.

Tom helped her up very carefully,
and said, "You can share my lunch with me."

She smiled and he did the same,

The Kindness Kitty felt pleased as she went on her way, to help spread more kindness to someone's day.

She saw some girls whispering and smirking, she knew something bad was lurking.

She walked along and just like that, took a seat right on their mat.

The little girls jumped with a fright,
"Who are you?" They asked with delight.

"I'm the Kindness Kitty" she said with a clap,
and jumped right onto the one girl's lap.

Then she asked, interrupting their chat,
"Who is that girl that you're pointing at?"

At once the girls began to say,

She started here the other day!

Her accent is weird, have you heard?

She doesn't understand a word!

"Something as simple as a smile, you'll find,
is a small thing that you can do to be kind.

The thing about a smile that is very unique,
is that a smile is understood
in whatever language you speak."

"We don't want to be kind," the girls said with a moan,
but the Kindness Kitty was cute, so they changed their tone.

One little girl, her name is Grace, put a big smile right across her whole face.

She walked up to the girl and said, "How are you?" And just like that the new girl smiled too!

They started to play and laugh in the sun,
and before they knew it play time was done.

The new girl's heart was happy and full,
it was the best day she'd ever had at school.

The Kindness Kitty walked away feeling good,
she wanted to help wherever she could.

Just like that she had a plan,
she saw a girl at the ice cream van.

Sally was yelling and going out of her mind,
because the ice cream she got
was not the right kind.

"I know what you can do with that." The Kindness Kitty said.
"Who are you?" Sally blushed, her face bright red.

"I'm the Kindness Kitty!" She said with a purr,
and jumped right up to where the ice creams were.

"If you give away something you don't want or need,
as easy as that you've done a kind deed."

"Over there you'll see a boy, he's never even owned a toy, he never has a proper meal, for him that ice cream would be a big deal."

"I'm not in the mood to be kind today," but the Kindness Kitty was cute so she listened anyway.

Sally walked over and without making a scene, she said to the boy,

The boy looked so happy, it made Sally feel great,
"I want to help more people and I don't want to wait!"

"I'm going to look for some things I have spare,
I'll give away toys and clothes for people to wear."

The Kindness Kitty was feeling so proud, that she started to PURRRRRRR very loud.

But as she came around the corner, she saw something new, it was the boy eating ice cream but looking quite blue.

She jumped onto his shoulder, "Hello Marty" she said,
he gave half a smile and scratched her on the head.

What's the matter with you today?

How can I be kind, if I have nothing to give away?

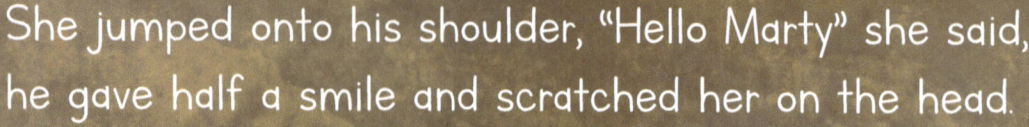

"Ah!" Said the Kindness Kitty looking very smart.

"You can be kind with your actions,
and with your heart."

"Kindness doesn't need to cost a thing, you see,
you can be kind with what you do and say for free."

"I don't know how to be kind," Marty said with a frown
but the Kindness Kitty was cute, so he couldn't let her down.

He looked up and just right there,
was a grumpy old lady, with silver-grey hair.

She was walking her dog on a summer's day, when all of a sudden, the dog ran away.

Just like that, he knew he should,
he ran after the dog as fast as he could.

He chased the dog all over the place,
the grumpy old lady had an angry look on her face.

Luckily Marty could run so fast,
he managed to catch the dog at last.

The old lady couldn't believe how kind Marty had been,
to help a stranger that he had never seen.

Then she did something she hadn't done in a while, the act of kindness made the old lady

SMILE.

but...

The one thing in common, one thing you will find,
something ALL of these people can be is...

KIND.

When you're kind to someone you will make their day,
and then they can spread kindness in their own special way.

Also by Stacy & Mira Reubenson

The Habit Rabbit teaches children good habits in fun and exciting ways.

Once the new habit sticks, The Habit Rabbit moves on to teach another child a good habit

www.ingramcontent.com/pod-product-compliance
Lightning Source LLC
Chambersburg PA
CBHW041203290426
44109CB00003B/110